OUTRAGEOUS WOMEN

Borgo Press Books Edited & Translated by FRANK J. MORLOCK

Anna Karenina: A Play in Five Acts, by Edmond Guiraud, from Leo Tolstoy
Anthony: A Play in Five Acts, by Alexandre Dumas, Père
The Children of Captain Grant: A Play in Five Acts, by Jules Verne and Adolphe d'Ennery
Crime and Punishment: A Play in Three Acts, by Frank J. Morlock, from Fyodor Dostoyevsky
Don Quixote: A Play in Three Acts, by Victorien Sardou, from Miguel de Cervantes
The Dream of a Summer Night: A Fantasy Play in Three Acts, by Paul Meurice
Falstaff: A Play in Four Acts, by William Shakespeare, John Dennis, William Kendrick, and Frank J. Morlock
The Idiot: A Play in Three Acts, by Frank J. Morlock, from Fyodor Dostoyevsky
Jesus of Nazareth: A Play in Three Acts, by Paul Demasy
The Jew of Venice: A Play in Five Acts, by Ferdinand Dugué
Joan of Arc: A Play in Five Acts, by Charles Desnoyer
The Lily of the Valley: A Play in Five Acts, by Théodore Barrière and Arthur de Beauplan, from Honoré de Balzac
Lord Byron in Venice: A Play in Three Acts, by Jacques Ancelot
Louis XIV and the Affair of the Poisons: A Play in Five Acts, by Victorien Sardou
The Man Who Saw the Devil: A Play in Two Acts, by Gaston Leroux
Mathias Sandorf: A Play in Three Acts, by Jules Verne and William Busnach
Michael Strogoff: A Play in Five Acts, by Jules Verne and Adolphe d'Ennery
Les Misérables: A Play in Two Acts, by Victor Hugo, Paul Meurice, and Charles Victor Hugo
The Mysteries of Paris: A Play in Five Acts, by Eugène Sue and Prosper Dinaux
Ninety-Three: A Play in Four Acts, by Victor Hugo and Paul Meurice
Notes from the Underground: A Play in Two Acts, by Frank J. Morlock, from Fyodor Dostoyevsky
Outrageous Women: Lady MacBeth and Other French Plays, edited by Frank J. Morlock
Peau de Chagrin: A Play in Five Acts, by Louis Judicis, from Honoré de Balzac
A Raw Youth: A Play in Five Acts, by Frank J. Morlock, from Fyodor Dostoyevsky
Richard Darlington: A Play in Three Acts, by Alexandre Dumas, Père
The San Felice: A Play in Five Acts, by Maurice Drack, from Alexander Dumas, Père
Saul and David: A Play in Five Acts, by Voltaire
Shylock, the Merchant of Venice: A Play in Three Acts, by Alfred de Vigny
Socrates: A Play in Three Acts, by Voltaire
The Stendhal Hamlet Scenarios and Other Shakespearean Shorts from the French, edited by Frank J. Morlock
A Summer Night's Dream: A Play in Three Acts, by Joseph-Bernard Rosier and Adolphe de Leuwen
Urbain Grandier and the Devils of Loudon: A Play in Four Acts, by Alexandre Dumas, Père
The Voyage Through the Impossible: A Play in Three Acts, by Jules Verne and Adolphe d'Ennery
The Whites and the Blues: A Play in Five Acts, by Alexandre Dumas, Père
William Shakespeare: A Play in Six Acts, by Ferdinand Dugué

OUTRAGEOUS WOMEN

Lady MacBeth and Other French Plays

Edited and Translated by

FRANK J. MORLOCK

THE BORGO PRESS

An Imprint of Wildside Press LLC

MMX

Copyright © 2002, 2010 by Frank J. Morlock

All rights reserved. No part of this book may be reproduced without the expressed written consent of the author. Professionals are warned that this material, being fully protected under the copyright laws of the United States of America, and all other countries of the Berne and Universal Copyright Convention, is subject to a royalty. All rights, including all forms of performance now existing or later invented, but not limited to professional, amateur, recording, motion picture, recitation, public reading, radio, television broadcasting, DVD, and Role Playing Games, and all rights of translation into foreign languages, are expressly reserved. Particular emphasis is placed on the question of readings, and all uses of these plays by educational institutions, permission for which must be secured in advance from the author's publisher, Wildside Press, 9710 Traville Gateway Dr. #234, Rockville, MD 20850 (phone 301-762-1305).

www.wildsidebooks.com

FIRST WILDSIDE EDITION

CONTENTS

Introduction, by Frank J. Morlock 7

Lady MacBeth, by Julius Le Sire 11

Zubiri, by Georges de Porto Riche 25

A False Conversation, by Théophile Gautier 55
  Scene I 59
  Scene II 77
  Scene III 91

Widow! by Henri Becque 97

About the Editor 113

DEDICATION

TO ALL THE OUTRAGEOUS WOMEN IN MY LIFE: YOU KNOW WHO YOU ARE!

INTRODUCTION

The French perfected one-act and short plays in the 1700s, long before similar short works became common on the English stage. The result, for a translator like myself, is finding a great deal of good dramatic material which is just too short to publish independently, and difficult to collect together in longer anthologies without finding some unifying theme.

I recently came across the play *Zubiri*, which is based on a tale that was either written by Victor Hugo, or was derived from an incident which he reported. I wanted to include it with a longer drama of Hugo's, but my publisher was afraid that it might get lost in the shadow of the better-known work. So he suggested putting together this anthology instead, since I had several other short pieces already in hand on the theme of the "Outrageous Woman."

Each of the ladies represented herein is outrageous in her own way. Lady MacBeth is power hungry, Zubiri is a cruel flirt, Celinda is flamboyant penitent for her sins, and Clotilde is a sly, controlling woman who manages to keep her love life under control even on the occasion of her husband's death.

The four plays run the gamut from tragedy to satire, from highly artificial comedy to Naturalism; and they present Eve, the Eternal Woman, in a variety of postures, none of them very flattering:

In *Lady MacBeth*, we have a guilt-ridden heroine who is nonetheless driven to rule.

In *Zubiri*, based on a report or tale by Victor Hugo, we are presented with a dancer-courtesan who torments her lover mercilessly by flirting in front of him shamelessly with his friends and likely successors to her charms, in one of the steamiest short pieces on record.

In Gautier's *A False Conversation*, Celinda, another dancer-courtesan, gives up the bright lights of Paris to follow a sham philosopher into a bucolic, Rousseau-like fantasy existence, only to discover that her sage is himself false.

And in *Widow!*, Clotilde is comforted by her

very discreet lover over the death of her unsuspecting husband.

I have been unable to discover much biographical information about Julius Le Sire. He seems to have begun writing under the First Empire, and penned an operetta, a cantata, and some essays. The dates of his birth and death remain unknown. But in *Lady MacBeth* he wrote a very effective and powerful study of guilt and ambition.

Théophile Gautier (1812-1872) was one of the leading Romanticists in France, being famous for wearing a red vest to the opening of *Hernani*. He is perhaps best known today as a drama critic and novelist, although he was also an innovative and highly underrated playwright. *A False Conversation* was written during his prime in 1846, but never performed during his lifetime, which now seems strange, since the play is easily staged and still very funny.

Georges de Porto Riche (1845-1930) was known before World War I as a playwright who often focused on his characters' passions. He is perhaps most famous for his short drama, *Françoise's Luck. Zubiri*, which was published in 1911, is astonishingly *risqué* for its time, but it was both published and performed contemporaneously. It was based on a "*récit*" by Victor Hugo (1802-1885), although I have been unable to locate the original in Hugo's collected works. In any event, it is different from most of the works for which Hugo is justifiably famous.

Henri Becque (1837-1899) first became famous with the staging of *Michel Pauper* in 1870. His best-known work today is *La Parisienne* (1885). *Widow!* is a marvelous character study of a woman who decides to get on with her life in the best way that she can.

None of these ladies are shrinking violets!

—Frank J. Morlock
San Miguel de Allende, México
October, 2009

LADY MacBETH

by Julius Le Sire

**TRANSLATED AND ADAPTED BY
FRANK J. MORLOCK**

CAST OF CHARACTERS

LADY MACBETH

A DOCTOR

A MAID

THE VOICE

LADY MacBETH

The stage represents the hall of a medieval castle. To the right, a table on which are a cushion of velour and a crown. To the left an armchair; back left, a table.

AT RISE, it is night. The clock strikes.

DOCTOR: By the King's orders, for the last two nights, I've been watching at the Queen's bedside, and the Queen is sleeping. Nothing has come to confirm your strange report and I doubt—

MAID: Wait, your science is wrong, for since King Macbeth went into the field to fight the English, the Queen rises at the slow striking of twelve at night, and, draping herself in her robes, slips from her bed. Then she does something strange, horrible, confused. Suddenly her voice changes, her expression relaxes, that's when she awakes.

DOCTOR: So then, she acts and speaks in her sleep?

MAID: (with terror) Look, look, she's coming. On my life, on my eternal soul, she's really asleep.

DOCTOR: It's a strange sleep. She speaks, she sees, and yet she's sleeping, because her body's acting.

MAID: She's coming, she's coming.

DOCTOR: Let's avoid her presence. Let us retire into the shadows and listen in silence.

(They withdraw.)

LADY MACBETH: (alone, entering slowly, holding a lamp in hand; her sleep is agitated; the clock strikes) The clock is striking. Midnight! I hear it without terror!

(as if speaking to someone present) You are trembling! A warrior, a Macbeth to be afraid! You are pale! What's become of your intrepid courage?

Press on, why forge ahead, will you, since my hand is guiding you.

(she puts down her lamp) My heart is beating to break out of my breast and death seems to freeze my voice! My eye is opening slowly with effort. Perhaps I am sleeping. The soul wakes and this eternal flame is not asleep.

(after a pause) The witches said, "Macbeth, you will be king." Dare extend your hand and don't tremble with fright. That old geezer that your heart environs with respect: He's not a mortal; he's only a crown. His life is the extinction of your fame. His life is slavery and obscurity for us. Go on! Duncan must die. You are trembling, O demented one. When you can strike a defenseless man what do you fear? Overwhelmed with exhaustion, Duncan is sleeping. Cease repeating that empty word "Virtue"! Virtue is only a word, a shadow, a vain phantom. In the end, what's a crime that pays for a kingdom? Chase away visions that trouble your spirit. Listen! Someone's coming! Why, no. It's midnight, it's midnight!

A VOICE: (singing offstage) It's midnight. Yes, it's midnight striking in the holy chapel

This hour recalls your actions to God. It's midnight! Exactly. Count this hour and sleep with joy. As for you, criminal, shiver and wake with terror. It's midnight.

LADY MACBETH: Fire spreads through my breast, a somber hope animates me. I'm leaving—because you are afraid, pusillanimous man! The crown is yours if you wish to seize it. You are letting it fall. It's up to me to finish it. Remember this word, revive your courage. This word, "You will be king"! repeated in the storm!— Ah, your face is clearing. At last I've reached you again. The savage light in your eyes, dagger in your hand.

(with joy) He's dead! He is dead. What a horrible sorrow comes to press my heart! Lord, is it possible that's remorse? No, no, it's not remorse. Ah, the scepter is ours since Duncan is dead! It's strange! In sleep he resembles my father! Shut my eyes then! Put out my light. He is no more! God what a scream! It's that of a stag. I didn't strike him; mine was not the blow. Macbeth, suspend your arm! It's I—I am your wife! I'm afraid! I'm afraid! I'm afraid! Throw that blade away. He's my father! Murderer begone! You horrify me. Parricide! Why, no. Pardon my error. I love you, O my

Macbeth, and wish that the world adore you on its knees. In my profound soul a single name's engraved—yours! It is my faith. O it's sweet to love. Reply, O my king! Who said that word to you? King! Indeed that's my dream. A furious delirium that never ends—torture of Hell full of fright, of terror that burns my flesh and tortures my heart. Tunic of Nessus stuck to your shoulders. Tunic that could contain the two poles, and yet it chokes me with its undulating folds. I want to tear it off, alas, my furious efforts are impotent, for the current drags me. Since Hell wishes it, well, so be it. Let's be Queen! Queen! Why Duncan lives—No—Macbeth struck him and the scepter, on that day, escaping from his hands, is going to fall into ours. A scepter, a crown. Remember well, Macbeth—It's I who gave them to you. Oh, I feel that I am dreaming and that I'm speaking aloud! From my desperate heart, despite me, the funereal revelation of my crime is escaping word by word. And on my paling face the terrifying secret is branded. It's read in my hands that I cannot wash. It's read in my eyes, and, to better accuse me, Duncan seems to raise his threatening head. Momentarily, he raises his dying eyelids. His virtuous eye illuminates, it burns my glance; his blood pours.

(with terror) He had so much blood, that old geezer! Blood—always blood. It isn't my blood. In that case what is it? Silence. Let's dry it. That's fine!

A VOICE: It's midnight. Mortals, pray! Implore clemency from heaven. From above God protects old and young. It's midnight. Just men, pray! From Heaven God reads in your heart. Criminal, repent and shiver with terror. It's midnight!

LADY MACBETH: Who's he talking to? Children? Threatening their lives? Is he envious of my maternal happiness? A crown on their heads is a beautiful ornament. And sparkles proudly on their blond hair. Yet more blood! The crown injures their heads. Ah, under its trefled gold memory arises! What to do to kill this somber memory! This incessant torture that never wants to end. To deflect the curse of God from me? I have so much need of blessing that I would like to pray. But God, in his wrath, makes prayer expire on my arid lips. Lord, I repent; Lord, I have faith in you! Pardon! No, no. I'm not lying, my heart had no terror. It conceived the crime. Back! Back, ghost! Yes, I wanted your death because I wanted your crown. Who placed the dagger in Macbeth's hand, who guided his uncertain and haggard eye? It was I. It was I. In a dark alcove is raised a royal bed full of mystery and shadow. That's where Duncan sleeps. A mysterious noise seems to hover in the air and to reign in these parts. Noiselessly and step by step a man gets there. He rears up; a woman follows him; she holds a lamp whose strange light infiltrates under the velour of the weakly lit canopy the curtain, the flame reddens. Striding for a moment, its light trembles over the lugubrious bed, pouring forth a bloody reflection. The wife is pale but her face is menacing. And in her eyes the furor in her soul can be read. She guides Macbeth's arm. That woman, that woman—she's me! I wanted power. It belongs to me! I have it! Horrible spectacle to view—a wave of blood springs from the breast of my victim. And on my reddened hand it imprints my crime. As with hot iron the executioner brands you. The stain's disappeared. No, no.

(with terror) It's staining the water.

(she rubs her hand)

A VOICE: It's midnight. At midnight remorse comes to torture your soul. Hear God the Avenger's voice which accuses you. It's midnight. Pray,

Christians, pray. Here's the angel of vengeance and his divine sword can strike you to the heart. It's midnight.

LADY MACBETH: Blood. Always this blood which chokes and oppresses me. It's climbing, climbing again. The vengeful wave already touches my lip. It's going to drown me. My strength is returning; I don't want to die! Always the odor of blood in the air that I breath, in the perfume of flowers, in the sighing wind. Blood. Let's dry it. The stain's disappeared. The accusatory sign is no more.

(with terror) It's reappearing!

(rubbing her hands) O stain from hell, miserable vestige of crime. Disappear, vanish I tell you. Nothing can erase it! Well, well, this iron I am going to burn my hand with; I'm going to burn my flesh. Nothing more.— Yes, there it is. Terrible torture. Enough, enough, I'm dying! Under your redoubtable hand I would like to awaken, for this dream is horrifying. Oh! To sleep without thinking—how lucky that must be, To sleep. To dream forever. Terrifying life: sinister hour, alas, followed by despair. Who will deliver me from this frightful torture? To whoever wakens me I will give my crown. I will give my power.

(waking up) Who spoke of the crown? Of this heavy burden? Finally, I'm waking! On my head heaven unfolds its splendors. Thus, everything is real. The crime, yes the crime, it is trickling down the walls. It's breaking my heart, tearing my entrails. In these foaming waves it's carrying off my life. But Scotland is my prey and I will reign still!

REFRAIN BY CHORUS

CURTAIN

ZUBIRI

by Georges de Porto Riche

From a Tale by Victor Hugo

**TRANSLATED AND ADAPTED BY
FRANK J. MORLOCK**

CAST OF CHARACTERS

SERIO

RODOLPHE

TEMPLIER

ZUBIRI

ZUBIRI

A private room in a Parisian Night Club circa 1845, at one o'clock in the morning. Flowers, rare wines, decorative plates. Lit candelabra on the table. Around the table, Serio and Templier chat while smoking. Rodolphe is seated at the piano.

TEMPLIER: (to Rodolphe) The Marseillais!

SERIO: Stop, it's forbidden.

RODOLPHE: (without ceasing to play) Right after the Three Braggarts.

(stopping) Say, there, Serio, the little lady is small but attractive.

TEMPLIER: The Italians closes before midnight

SERIO: (with jealousy) Her ballet is over at ten thirty.

RODOLPHE: Suppose you go get her.

SERIO: She doesn't like me to go backstage.

TEMPLIER: Isn't he obedient.

RODOLPHE: Bet she beats him.

SERIO: (gravely) It's truer than you think.

TEMPLIER: (cocking his ear) Here she is.

SERIO: (joyfully) I recognize the swish of her skirts.

(Zubiri appears in a sumptuous and disordered outfit)

ZUBIRI: (gaily) I was just molested by a woman.

RODOLPHE: By a woman?

ZUBIRI: Very pretty, my word. She rushed up to me in the wings and planted a kiss on my neck.

SERIO: (jealously) The slut!

ZUBIRI: Well, what of it. It wasn't a man!

RODOLPHE: (helping her with her cloak) Little Zubiri, look at the clock.

ZUBIRI: You should have begun without me.

(to Serio) I'm late?

SERIO: I don't think so.

TEMPLIER: Gutless.

ZUBIRI: (to Serio) Now, not a word, and sit down there.

SERIO: (sitting close to her) Not so far away.

(They all install themselves around the table and begin to dine.)

ZUBIRI: (to Templier) As for you, sir, place yourself near me and don't play footsie. You mustn't betray the dunce. If you knew the truth, I'm the one who's dumb. I love him. You see he's very ugly.

RODOLPHE: (pulling apart a chicken) Not all that much.

ZUBIRI: (sitting between Templier and Serio) It's true he has some talent; great talent, even, but conceive that he got me in a comic manner. I'd seen him prowling around backstage for some time, and I said, "Who's this gentleman who's so ugly?" I said that to Prince Capristi who brought him to supper one night. When I saw him up close, I said: It's a monkey. He looked at me, I don't know why. At the end of the supper, I pressed his hand when giving him a napkin. As he took leave of me, he whispered, "What day would you like me to come to you?" I replied. "What? Don't come during the day, you are too ugly. Come at night. He came one night. I put out all the candles. He came the next day again, the day after that, like this for three nights. I didn't know what I had.

(to Templier who offers her something to drink) No champagne, I prefer Burgundy.

(resuming) The fourth day, I said to my piano teacher, "I don't know what I've got. There's a man that I don't know, I actually don't know his name. He takes my head on his breast, and then he speaks softly to me, so gently. He's very poor, he doesn't have a sou. He has two sisters who are nothing. He's ill, he has palpitations.

(Serio gestures in acquiescence)

A bit too many palpitations! I'm doglike scared of being madly in love with him." My piano mistress said to me, "Bah!" The fifth day it seemed to me that he was going to leave. I said to my piano mistress, "Why, he's starting to love me a lot, this gentleman." I didn't know at all where I was. Sir, this lasted more than thirty-two days. And imagine: he doesn't sleep. He's a man who doesn't sleep, so in the morning, I kick him out with big kicks.

SERIO: (very low) It's true, she kicks like a horse.

ZUBIRI: (to Rodolphe) But, sir. You are letting me die of thirst.

TEMPLIER: (pouring her a drink) Here's some Chamberton.

ZUBIRI: (To Serio) You are truly too ugly, you see to have a woman like me.

(To Templier) Indeed, sir, you cannot judge me; my shape's a bit rumpled, that's all. But I really have many pretty things about me. Say there, Serio, would you like me to show him my throat?

SERIO: (going pale) Go Ahead!

(Slowly, with a hesitating and flirtatious gesture, Zubiri removes her half-open dress, questioning Serio with adoring eyes and a mocking smile)

ZUBIRI: What's it do to you, when I show him my throat, say, Serio? He really has to see it. For, since one of these days I'll belong to him. I'm going to show him. Want me to?

SERIO: (submissive and furious) Go ahead!

ZUBIRI: (bursting into laughter) Heavens! Suppose he sees my throat, Serio? Everybody's seen it. Huh? Those ladies at the Comédie Française who have breasts like these for you.

(She grasps her dress firmly with both hands, leans forward, and lets her cleavage be seen)

SERIO: (jealous, but scornful) Why, look, will you, at the cleavage of a virgin, and the smile of a child.

ZUBIRI: (already a little drunk) Ah, you know indeed that I love you. Don't be annoyed. Because up to now you've only had old women. You are not accustomed to the rest of us, by Jove. It's all simple, your old ones, they have nothing to show.

(sitting on his lap)

It's true, my poor lad. You as yet have had only old women. You are all so ugly! Well do you want them to show you your Princess of Belle Joyeuse, that spectre! Your Countess d'Argota, that witch! And your great devil of a blue-stocking of fifty-five years, who has bleached blonde hair, and promises you the Institute! Look, my love, which do you prefer—a chair in the Academy or the chaise-longue of your mistress?

SERIO: (proudly) Your hair is undone.

ZUBIRI: And I'm losing my slipper.

(Templier gives her her slipper)

SERIO: (jealously) Templier—

ZUBIRI: (to Templier as she pushes her hair back) Thanks, sir.

(sings)

She was barefoot,
Her hair was undone.

(Rodolphe gets up from the table and goes to the piano)

ZUBIRI: (singing)

She was barefoot
Her hair was undone.
Seated, barefoot, among the leaning bushes
I passing by there, methought I saw a fairy,
And I said to her: "Would you like to come into the fields?"

(interrupting herself)

Would you? Would you?

(resuming the song)

She looked at me with a haughty look
Which remains beautiful even as it triumphs over us.
And I said to her, I said, "Would you? It's the season in which one loves.
Would you like for us to go under the thick trees?

(interrupting herself, to Rodolphe)

Would you? Would you?

Heavens, one of my little combs has slipped down my back.

(resuming the song)

She dried her feet on the grass by the shore
She looked at me for the second time.
And the beautiful wanton suddenly became pensive.
Oh, how the birds sing in the depths of the woods.
How the water gently lapped the shore.
I see coming to me in great green reeds
The beautiful girl, happy, frightened and wild
Her hair in her eyes and laughing broadly.

SERIO: (distracted) I love you, Zubiri.

RODOLPHE: Beware of Madame Viardot.

ZUBIRI: Find my comb, sir.

SERIO: (begging) Zubiri.

ZUBIRI: (to Templier, who slips his hand between her shoulders) Lower, under my chemise.

SERIO: (raising his fist to Templier) Sir!

ZUBIRI: (to Serio) Paws down!

RODOLPHE : You are murdering him, Zubiri!

ZUBIRI: (cynically) He nearly killed me last night.

(sings)

She was barefoot—

(to Templier)

Stop tickling me.

SERIO: (in despair) Zubiri.

TEMPLIER: (fumbling in Zubiri's back) I've got it.

SERIO: Why, Zubiri?

ZUBIRI: (singing) Her hair was undone—

SERIO: Zubiri.

(he slips from his chair in a faint)

ZUBIRI: (rushing to Serio) What's wrong? Are you dumb!

(rubbing his hands and throwing water on his face. Serio reopens his eyes. Zubiri sits at his feet and holds his hands)

This slob! To get ill because I show my neck. Ah, indeed, if he's known me just six months ago he would have had fainting fits. But still, he's not a cretin. You know Zarbaza did a nude portrait of me.

SERIO: Yes, and he made a fat woman heavy, a Fleming; it's quite bad.

ZUBIRI: He's an animal, and as I didn't have money to pay for the portrait at this very moment he's offering to I don't know who in exchange for a clock. Well, you see plainly, you don't need to get angry. It's only a woman's neck—and what's the rest, anyway? besides, it's certain that your friend will be my lover after you, you see. Oh, at this moment, here, sir, I couldn't. If you were Louis XIV. Still, I couldn't do it. If they gave me fifty thousand francs I couldn't deceive Serio. Hold on, I have Prince Capristi who will return one of these days. You know, there's always a backlog of business. And still, there are some folks who want me. There are always some who are curious and have money, who say: "Here, I want to spend the night with this little rat, with this creature, with this girl, with these eyes, with these shoulders, with this effrontery, with this cynicism. It must be amusing to see this Zubiri up close; she dances so nicely." I am used to Capristi. Sir, when Capristi returns I won't be able to endure him for ten minutes; if he remains a quarter of an hour, I will kill him.

RODOLPHE: Many things can be done in ten minutes.

ZUBIRI: (surrounding Serio in her arms and buttoning the collar of his shirt) Is he a slob to be ill and scare me like that? Ah, here's what will set him up again right away.

(finding flowers on his chest) Heavens, you kept my flowers?

SERIO: (bitterly) I am quite sure you haven't kept mine.

ZUBIRI: Ingrate! I hid them in a little box that I got for my first Communion.

SERIO: Seriously?

ZUBIRI: (brandishing the flowers) He's the one who picked them for me the day before yesterday, on the rocks of Saint Adiesse. The wind was blowing in a terrible way. I stayed a hundred meters back. I thought that the storm was going to carry him off.

RODOLPHE: Him!

ZUBIRI: Yes, him, despite his big body.

(declaiming)

I picked this flower for you on the hill,
On the bitter escarpment on which the waves break
That only the eagle knows and can get close to
Peaceably, it crosses the chinks in the rocks,
Shade bathes the flanks of the dismal promontory.
I saw, as one decorates a place of victory
A large Arch of Triumph, blazing and vermillion
In the place where the Sun was engulfed.
The shaded night erected a porch of clouds,
Veils fled away, diminished in the distance.
Some roofs lit up in the depth of the funnel
Seeming afraid to shine and of allowing themselves
  to be seen.

(interrupting herself)

A little severe, this story.

RODOLPHE: Don't stop.

ZUBIRI: My professor said that if Rachel heard me she would be jealous.

SERIO: For sure.

(Zubiri extends her glass to Templier)

TEMPLIER: More Burgundy?

ZUBIRI: (drinking) It's more gay.

(continuing to declaim)

I picked this flower for you, my beloved
It's pale and has no embalmed corolla
Its seed doesn't grow on the crest of mountains.
Only the bitter smell of sea-green seaweed,
As for me, I said: Poor flower from the height of this peak
You must go into an immense abyss
Where algae, clouds, and sails go.
Go die on a heart, an abyss more deep
Fade on this breast on which a world palpitates
Heaven which created you to flower in the sea
Made you for ocean; I give you to love.
The wind shuffles the waves; of day there remains
Only a vague light, slowly erased.
Oh, how sad I was in the depth of my thought
While I was thinking and the black abyss
Dragged me into its soul with all the evening shivers.

TEMPLIER: Bravo!

RODOLPHE: Little Zubiri, you've got talent.

TEMPLIER: How moving her voice is.

SERIO: I love you, Zubiri.

ZUBIRI: (caressingly) Oh my poor old thing, I love you, too.

(to Templier) Sir, he wakes me every night at four o'clock in the morning, and tells me of his family and his poverty, and of his huge table that he made for The Council of State. After that, he gets pissed off with me, with his jeremiads; it's probably some nonsense he had with old women. All men are such scoundrels! I am quite stupid to let myself be captivated by all that, right? All the same it captivates me. I think of him during the day—that's bizarre. But it's because I am in love with what's nice.— In love with this little monkey.

SERIO: Zubiri.

ZUBIRI: Yes, gentlemen, with this monkey of a Serio. Finally, imagine that I call him my mother, yes, my mother. Even when I am in his arms. But at moments when I am completely sad.

(to Templier) Still, a little wine.

(continuing) Do you know? I want to die! Indeed, I'm going to be twenty-four years old; I'm going to get old, too, I am. What's the good of shriveling up, fading, and falling apart, little by little?

It's better to go suddenly
At least that's what some loafers who smoke their
   cigars outside Tortoni's say.
Heavens, you know this pretty girl? She's dead

When later, they'd say: So, she's finally dead, that frightful old witch. What's the use for her to live like that? It's boring. Now these are the elegies I make myself. So you see, I've decided to die young. I don't want to pass twenty-five. It's agreed between the Pope and me.

SERIO: Like the little Maillard.

RODOLPHE: The poor thing had beautiful eyes.

TEMPLIER: But her knees were pointed.

ZUBIRI: You hear, Serio?

RODOLPHE: Pass on again. Day under the dress, but at night, under the bed covers, when one is right next to each other.

TEMPLIER: One catches the blues.

ZUBIRI: If you imagine men don't cause them. I wear on my left ass what I owe this wretch who's heavy as a hundred pound crown.

(she pulls up her dress) Judge for yourself.

SERIO: (furious) Zubiri.

ZUBIRI: (to Templier) First of all, sir, you have not yet seen my leg up close. You only know my dancer's leg; you are going to admire my woman's leg.

SERIO: (beside himself) Zubiri!

ZUBIRI: (placing her half naked leg on the table clothe) Sir, I forbid you to say to your Club that my knee is pointed. You mustn't make up lies. Agree it's round and shiny like the skull of my Capuchin uncle.— Now there's one who loves love.

SERIO: (begging) Zubiri!

RODOLPHE: (examining Zubiri's leg) And this famous bruise. I don't see it.

ZUBIRI: (standing on the table) The blue mark he caused me! Here it is, up higher. Higher than my garter. Put a kiss on it.

RODOLPHE: (obeying) Thanks.

SERIO: Zubiri.

ZUBIRI: (softening over herself and hugging her leg) My sweet little ass.

SERIO: Zubiri

ZUBIRI: (proposing her leg to Templier) And you, too, sir.

TEMPLIER: (kissing her leg) What's your perfume?

ZUBIRI: (standing on the table) Verbena.

SERIO: Zubiri!

ZUBIRI: (completely drunk) Shut up, cruel man

(a piano can be heard; she cocks her ear) Why, it's the Esmeralda they're strumming on that side. I danced that figure in Naples, at San Carlo, I recall.

(softened) Perhaps someone's behind this wall thinking of me. I thank you, sir, I really love men that I don't know.

(blowing a kiss to the wall and dancing on the table) What a shame to be wearing such a long skirt.

(she hitches up her dress and starts to dance.)

SERIO: (ready to faint) Zubiri.

ZUBIRI: (continuing to dance) Bah! What do you care if they look at my leg, since you'll have me all to yourself in an hour. All the same, sooner or later, these gentlemen will possess it, too, just like you; my leg belongs to France!

SERIO: (despairing) Zubiri!

ZUBIRI: (to Serio who removes the candelabra from the table) Very good; remove the candelabra or I'm going to burn my—only hope of fortune.

SERIO: (begging) Zubiri.

ZUBIRI: (calling off) Hey, neighbor, not so fast! You are there! Great!

(she dances with more and more effrontery)

SERIO: Zubiri

(Suddenly, she trips in her skirts and falls into Rodolphe's arms)

ZUBIRI: (sitting on Rodolphe's shoulder and declaiming madly as the music plays in a muffled way)

If you like, let's make a dream
Let's mount on two palfreys
You will lead me; I will carry you away.
The bird is singing in the woods!

RODOLPHE: (in the same tone) I am your master and your prey.

ZUBIRI: Let's leave, the day is over.

(pointing to Serio) My nag will be joyful.

TEMPLIER: (pointing to Serio) Your horse will be love!

SERIO: Zubiri.

ZUBIRI:

We'll make their heads touch.
Travels are easy.
We will give these animals
A barn full of kisses.

(She surrounds Rodolphe in her arms and plants a kiss on his mouth.)

SERIO: (in an extinguished voice) Zubiri!

ZUBIRI: (her glass in her hand)

Come, be tender, I am drunk

O the green brush is soaked
Your breath will make you follow
The wakened butterflies.

SERIO: Zubiri.

ZUBIRI: (more and more carried away)

Let's go by way of Australia
We'll have dawn in our face.
I will be great and you will be rich
Since we love each other.

SERIO: Zubiri!

ZUBIRI:

We'll go to an inn
And we'll pay the innkeeper
With your virgin smile
And my scholarly "Hello."

RODOLPHE: (kissing her) With my scholarly "Hello."

SERIO: (slipping from his chair and falling to the ground) Zubiri.

ZUBIRI: (leaping from the table and running to him.) What's wrong this time? You are pale again? Serio!

TEMPLIER: This time he's really fainted.

RODOLPHE: (gravely) I think he's dead.

ZUBIRI: Dead? Come on, you're mad! Every evening, I'm present at the same tragedy. Serio! Serio!

(on her knees beside him, with love, with despair) Open your eyes again, my tender friend. I accept that you are ill, but I don't want you to die. You know that very well. Come on, we'll finish this joke—and take me in your arms like this morning.

RODOLPHE: (considering Serio) His arm is falling back.

ZUBIRI: (weeping over the body of Serio) Oh! You won't cause me this pain. Remember the good kisses that I gave you. You will see. I'm keeping better ones for you. You aren't moving, Serio!

TEMPLIER: He's the second one she's killed.

ZUBIRI: Dead!

(the piano in the next room can be heard. With distraction and a falling voice)

The melody still drags on.
Under the trees blued by the serene morn.
Then tremble, then expire, and the voice that sang
Extinguishes like a bird resting. All is quiet.

(She rises and sits down again, and weeps, her face hidden in a napkin.)

CURTAIN

A FALSE CONVERSATION

or,

GOOD BLOOD NEVER LIES

by Théophile Gautier

**TRANSLATED AND ADAPTED BY
FRANK J. MORLOCK**

CAST OF CHARACTERS

FLORINE
DUKE
CHEVALIER
MR. DE VANDORE
COMMANDER
MARQUIS
CELINDA
ROSIMENE
ST. ALBIN
SUZON

A FALSE CONVERSATION

SCENE I.

FLORINE: My dear lords, I can only repeat to you what I've already said. My mistress is not here.

DUKE: That is the utmost falsity. I saw her leaning out of her window.

CHEVALIER: I will only believe she's not here if she comes to tell us so herself.

DUKE: Does she take us for creditors or men of letters, who come to offer their dedications?

DE VANDORE: We are not jokers or scoundrels. Those appellations are not our concern. Gentlemen, you don't know the correct way of questioning serving girls.

(pulling out his purse) Now, Florine, be frank, is your mistress home?

FLORINE: Yes, sir.

DE VANDORE: I knew quite well I'd get her to speak.

CHEVALIER: How cruel to conceal herself from friends like us who have never missed one of her suppers. What ingratitude!

DE VANDORE: Have us in, little one.

FLORINE: Your eloquence is, indeed, persuasive, sir. But I find myself, much to my regret, forced to keep your purse without opening the door to you.

DE VANDORE: For God's sake, Florine. You are worse than Cerberus. You take the gift, but you don't allow anyone to pass!

FLORINE: I know my duty.

DUKE: Since this is the way things stand, I've decided to lay siege to the house. I am going to dig a tunnel under the gate or tunnel a mine right into

Celinda's alcove. I know where it is, thank God.

FLORINE: The Duke is a terrible man.

DE VANDORE: (aside) I really want to return to pay court to Rosimene. It's true, she's received me very coldly. To be pushed out or not to be admitted—the chance being equal—I'll stay. My God, in a century of conception, it's difficult to have an affair of the heart.

CHEVALIER: Come on, Florine. Don't be strict with us. It's not like you to be cruel.

FLORINE: You like to have things repeated. My mistress is here, it's true. But it is as if she weren't. Madame does not wish to receive anyone. Neither today, nor tomorrow, nor the day after. She's determined. From now on, we shall live far from the noise of the world in an inaccessible solitude.

DUKE: We'll put things straight. We don't wish to spend our lives dying of boredom. We will pursue Celinda until the end of her odyssey. What the devil! After having shown her friends such a pretty face, full of lilies and roses, one cannot make them kiss a face of oak studded with steel nails.

COMMANDER: Celinda, the pearl of our suppers. Celinda, who so cheerfully wet her pretty, rosy lips in the foam of champagne less sparkling than she.

MARQUIS: Celinda, who sang so well, verses over dessert which amused us so much! Celinda, this smile of our joy, this star of our mad nights.

CHEVALIER: She's retiring from the world.

DUKE: She, a hermit—and virtuous!

CHEVALIER: It's ignoble.

DUKE: It's monstrous.

DE VANDORE: What will she do, shut up like that? How will she pass the time?

FLORINE: We will read *The Social Contract* and we will study philosophy.

COMMANDER: I will wager your philosophy has mustaches and spurs.

MARQUIS: Celinda is in love with a Negro or a

poet—at the least.

DUKE: What an example of her type.

CHEVALIER: Bah! Celinda is a girl who has sentiments and who only likes good things. It's a caprice which cannot last.

COMMANDER: What will we do to ruin ourselves?

MARQUIS: She had an inventive fantasy to dry up, in a year, the richest vein of mines in Peru. We must now find a way of spending our money ourselves. Her absence will be cruelly felt. You won't believe me, because it is so ridiculous, but is' more than fifteen years since I have—I don't know what to do with my money. Hey, Duke, do you want me to loan you a thousand pounds?

DUKE: Thanks, I am gambling from noon to midnight to save myself from a pecuniary congestion.

MARQUIS: We must be careful. The situation is grave. See rather this great financier: he's stuffed with pounds, doubloons up to his blazoned throat, contending with all the troubles of the world. He'll explode one of these days. He'll die of melted gold.

DUKE: Only Celinda can prevent such misfortunes.

CHEVALIER: What shall we do with ourselves today?

DUKE: Faith, I don't know, my boy. I had set myself on the idea of spending the evening with Celinda. Devil if I can think of an alternative.

COMMANDER: By God, let's stay. If Celinda doesn't want to be here, it's not our fault. We are almost at home here, anyway.

DUKE: I gave her the house.

COMMANDER: I bought the furniture.

MARQUIS: I, the livery and the carriages.

CHEVALIER: We're here in a hotel—furnished.

ALL: By us.

COMMANDER: Let's stay.

CHEVALIER: Here are cards. Let's play whist.

FLORINE: What are you thinking of, gentlemen? You are forgetting you are not at home.

DUKE: On, the contrary, my sweet, we are remembering. What's the stake, Chevalier?

CHEVALIER: A gold crown, to begin.

FLORINE: Gentlemen, please.

CHEVALIER: If you say one more word, Florine, we'll make you kiss Mr. de Vandore, who is at his absolute ugliest today.

FLORINE: I give up. I'm going to tell my mistress what is happening.

DUKE: It would really be a crime to allow a pretty thing like Celinda to adopt the customs of savages and goths—let's keep her, despite herself, on the right path—and not permit her to deviate from the traditions of an elegant lifestyle.

CHEVALIER: Here she is herself, our obstinacy had its effect.

(Enter Celinda.)

DUKE: Well, beautiful, here you are again. Here you see a Duke, a Marquis, a Commander, a Chevalier, and even a financier who are dying in your absence. Where does this savage cruelty come from that renders you insensible to the sighs of such adorers? This poor Chevalier has lost what little sense he had. He neglects himself and doesn't curl his hair more than three times a day—and wears the same watch for a week. He's a lost man.

CELINDA: Sir, stop your joking. I am not in the mood to endure it. And, tell me why you remain in my house by force and against my orders? Is it because I am a dancer and you are a Duke?

DUKE: My despair has made me impolite. Having no other way, I took it.

CHEVALIER: You are lacking in respect to all Paris.

COMMANDER: The universe is very embarrassed in its person and doesn't know what to do.

DUKE: If you knew how stupid de Vandore has

become since he no longer sees you.

CELINDA: You absolutely want me to leave. This obstinacy is strange. To want to visit people despite themselves!

COMMANDER: Bad girl! Can anyone live without you?

CELINDA: I assure you that I have not the least wish to see you and that I will never break down your door. Please leave, it's the only pleasure you could give me.

DE VANDORE: (aside) Oh, the little demon! Decidedly, I won't speak to her of my Florine, and I'll keep for a better time this little song I wrote on the back of a fifty thousand pound bank draft which I brought specially in my pocket. I think, really, that Rosimene is still in a mood less harsh. I feel I don't know what desire to return there.

CHEVALIER: This is unfriendly. To treat us this way, your best friends.

CELINDA: You are not my friends, I hope, although you fill my house. Henceforth, my days shall be in a retreat. I never want to see anyone again.

DUKE: "Anyone," right? But, I'm someone.

CELINDA: Let me live the way I fancy. Forget me. That won't be difficult for you. Enough others will replace me. You have Dupline, Fausena, Lendameny, the whole of the opera, the comedy. They will receive you with open arms. I've amused you enough. I've sung enough, danced enough, at your parties and suppers. What do you want from me? You've had my gaiety, my smile, my beauty, my talent. Can I take them away from you? You knew how to pay for all this with handfuls of gold. What does it matter to me how bored you are? Besides, I wouldn't amuse you any more. My character has totally changed. I've felt the emptiness of this brilliant frivolity. From having known others too much, the taste for simple pleasures has come to me. I want to reflect and think. That's enough to tell you there can no longer be anything in common between us.

CHEVALIER: Is it Celinda who's talking this way?

CELINDA: Yes, me! What's so surprising in that? It no longer pleases me to laugh. I don't laugh. I no longer wish to see anyone. I shut my door. That's all.

COMMANDER: What a singular caprice—to extinguish at the moment of its greatest luster, one of the most luminous stars in the heaven of the Opera.

CELINDA: Nothing could be simpler. I diverted you and you did not divert me. Do you think, Duke, that it is so agreeable to see the Marquis for an entire evening slouching in an armchair, dangling his legs, pulling a little mirror from his pocket, and making the cutest faces at himself.

DUKE: Indeed, it's not very gay.

CELINDA: And you, Chevalier, do you find the Duke, who only speaks of his hounds, his horses and his carriages, and who is in love with everything regarding the stable, a very entertaining person? That would drive an English groom to despair.

CHEVALIER: It's true that conversation is not the Duke's forte.

CELINDA: Commander, you are but the shadow of yourself. Your principal merit consists in being a great eater and a great drinker. You're not a man, you're a stomach. You've become a turkey, and only six bottles trouble your head. You go to sleep after dinner. Well, sleep at home.

DE VANDORE: How deceiving appearances are. I, who thought her so sweet and charming.

CELINDA: As for Mr. de Vandore, he's a sack of money with clothes and lace. Let him hide it in a strong box. That's his plan.

ALL: Well said, well said. She always had a devilish wit.

DUKE: You don't wish to come to Marly?

CELINDA: No.

CHEVALIER: At the musical concert being given where one hears this famous foreign singer—

CELINDA: No, I tell you.

COMMANDER: I've just received from Perigord

certain truffles which are not bad, washed down with a little wine, I have, in a corner of my wine cellar known to me alone— Come, sup with us.

CELINDA: No, no, a thousand times no. I no longer wish to live with strawberries and cream. All your poisoned dishes don't tempt me.

COMMANDER: Poisoned dishes! Truffles of the first choice! Don't repeat what you just said or you will lose your reputation. For you to hold such strange opinions, something strange must have happened to your wits. You've been reading bad books, or you are amorous—which is in bad taste and good only for dressmakers.

CELINDA: They won't go! If they should meet St. Albin!

DUKE: You are burning with an impure love for someone of questionable birth that you dare not produce. A shop boy, a soldier, a newspaper man. Take care, Celinda, you cannot descend below a Baron. You must be a Duchess or a Queen to permit yourself the caprice of a lackey or a poet— without there being evil consequences. All that I say to you is in your interest. Gentlemen, since Celinda is so inhospitable today, come spend the evening with me. We will drink. And for desert, Lindamuso and Rosimene will dance on the table to the accompaniment of broken glasses. Madame, I cast my regrets at your feet.

DE VANDORE: I still want to slip my stanzas to her—

(All exit except Celinda.)

CELINDA: Gone at last! That was difficult. They were used to being more at home here than in their own homes. Ah, my dear Marquis, how I hate you with all my soul. They were born insolent. Why didn't I notice it until today? They were always this way. I alone have changed. Celinda— Celinda is no more. A new woman has been born in me. Since I read Rousseau, my eyes have opened. I've never loved. I'd never met St. Albin. That young man with an honest soul, with an enthusiastic heart, who declaims so eloquently in my boudoir, of the corruption of cities, and the innocence of rural life. If these imbeciles had known how I adore a young preceptor named, quite simply, St. Albin, who doesn't even powder his hair—there would be so many taunts, so many jibes. But, time presses. Tonight, I must break these bonds. I've written the management breaking my engagement. Let's return these presents, the rewards of guilty weaknesses.

(ringing) Florine, take this bracelet back to the Duke and this choker to the Chevalier.

(St. Albin enters.)

CELINDA: Finally! I thought you weren't coming.

ST. ALBIN: I'm early.

CELINDA: My heart is always ahead of time. No one saw you?

ST. ALBIN: No one. The street was deserted.

CELINDA: It's not that I blush over you—even were you a Duke or slave trader—but I fear for my happiness. Our great dull Lords would never pardon me for being happy.

ST. ALBIN: Are you still surrounded by their obsessions?

CELINDA: Still! But, I've taken my leave. For you, I abandon glory, the stage, fortune. I am leaving the theatre.

ST. ALBIN: You are renouncing the Opera.

CELINDA: It bores me to live in clouds and mythological glories. I abdicate. From goddess, I've become a woman again. I will only be beautiful for you, sir.

ST. ALBIN: How can I show gratitude for such an act of love?

CELINDA: Rehearsals will no longer disturb our meetings. We will have forever to love each other.

ST. ALBIN: Yes, my all-beautiful. Twenty-four hours a day is not enough.

CELINDA: We will live in the country, all by ourselves in a little cottage. We will realize Rousseau's ideal. We'll have cows that I will milk myself.

ST. ALBIN: It will be charming. You've understood me. The pastoral life has always been my dream.

CELINDA: Sundays, we'll dance with the villagers. I'll wear a simple ribbon in my hair.

ST. ALBIN: But, you mustn't forget yourself and execute a pirouette or do a bump and grind.

CELINDA: Have no fear. I will quickly forget the graceful footwork. I was born to be a shepherdess.

ST. ALBIN: To feel the earth, to watch the flocks. That's the true destiny of man. Paris, city of mud and smoke, I shall leave you forever.

CELINDA: Let us flee far from a corrupt society.

ST. ALBIN: I've already had some clothes made. The village tailors are so clumsy. But, who cares about the cut of one's suit? Virtue alone makes a man happy.

CELINDA: Virtue, accompanied by a little love. Come, darling, my carriage is waiting.

ST. ALBIN: I have to write the family whose children I am raising after Rousseau's methods of an imperious necessity which forces me to renounce these philosophic duties.

CELINDA: Perhaps, in our retreat you will have the opportunity to exercise your talents. Ah, I will not be an unnatural mother. Our child will not suck mercenary milk.

(They leave.)

BLACKOUT

A FALSE CONVERSATION

SCENE II.

A month later. A hermitage near Montmorency.

ST. ALBIN: How will you dress to go to this country feast? There will be some city women there. Will you wear your diamonds?

CELINDA: The flowers of the field will be my diamonds. I don't want those gorgeous ornaments which make me remember what I ought to forget. I've sent back the jewels to those who gave them to me.

ST. ALBIN:

Sublime!

(aside) It's a shame. I loved the blue lights that the stones gave off in the candlelight.

(aloud) And your lace?

CELINDA: Sold. I gave the money to the poor. They'd be torn to pieces by the thorns of bushes and roses.

ST. ALBIN: Lace is really nice at the end of a dress.

CELINDA: Shall I drag my skirt in prairie dust? A dress of English cotton, streaked with red, a straw hat. That will be my outfit.

ST. ALBIN: You must put on a little rouge. You are pale.

CELINDA: The crystal water of the springs will suffice to revive color in my cheeks.

ST. ALBIN: I am still of the opinion that a touch of rouge under the eye lights up your face, and a bit of lipstick. Are you bringing your perfume? The villagers sometimes have a strong odor.

CELINDA: Violets on my breast will be my only perfume.

ST. ALBIN: I appreciate the violets, but perfume has its charm.

CELINDA: A perfidious charm which intoxicates and disturbs. Nature disdains all such vain refinements.

ST. ALBIN: Come as you like. You will always be pretty. (taking his hat)

CELINDA: Are you going out again?

ST. ALBIN: I haven't put a foot outside for ages.

CELINDA: You were gone all day yesterday.

ST. ALBIN: Was it yesterday I went to Paris? It seems so long ago.

CELINDA: What you said was not very gallant.

ST. ALBIN: You really have a bad disposition. I spoke without thinking. Goodbye. I am going for a walk and, in the depths of the forest, I'll meditate the true way of making people happy.

(Exit St. Albin. Enter Florine.)

FLORINE: Oh, that wicked beast of a cow! She ran right off with my bonnet and knocked over a pail of milk in the stable. We won't have any cream to make cheese and we'll have to go two leagues to get some elsewhere. Long live Paris, where you can get what you want.

CELINDA: (dreaming) The Opera must be playing today.

FLORINE: Yes. And Rosimene is dancing your dances.

CELINDA: Rosimene—dancing my dances. A creature like that. Only good enough to play in the chorus.

FLORINE: She's intrigued a lot. Now she's the lead dancer.

CELINDA: Who told you that? It's impossible.

FLORINE: You know that young painter who

likes me. I met him the other day and he persuaded me to pose for him—as a wood nymph. While I was posing, he told me all the scandals of the green room.

CELINDA: But she's all superficiality. She's stolen two balusters from some balcony to make her legs.

FLORINE: De Vandore has done mad things for her. He gave her a hotel in the suburbs. And magnificent plate, and the other day, she was in a carriage with four horses and an enormous coachman and three gigantic lackeys running behind. A train for a Princess of the blood.

CELINDA: She's a horror. She's a bit of flesh held together with hooks and eyes and corsets.

FLORINE: When I think that madame, who is so well made, has buried herself completely in a frightful desert for love of a small young man, handsome enough it is true, but without the least stability.

CELINDA: (frightened) Florine, Florine, look!

FLORINE: What's wrong?

CELINDA: A toad has come in through the open door and comes skipping over the floor.

FLORINE: The frightful beast! With his big popping eyes, he frightfully resembles Mr. de Vandore.

CELINDA: I am going to faint. Florine, don't abandon me in this extreme peril.

FLORINE: Where are the tongs? I can catch him by a paw and throw him delicately over the wall.

CELINDA: Take care he doesn't hurl his venom in your face.

FLORINE: Fear nothing. I am brave. Soon we'll be rid of this importunate visitor.

CELINDA: I breathe. The description of hermitages by authors do not speak of toads who want to slide into your privacy.

FLORINE: I always told you, madame, that authors are imbeciles. The country is made for peasants, and not for persons well brought up.

CELINDA: Good God! A wasp is buzzing against the window. If it were to sting me!

FLORINE: With two or three passes with my handkerchief, I am going to try to make him fall to the ground. We'll crush him then.

(Florine kills the wasp.)

CELINDA: What perils! It's frightful to be pursued this way by evil animals. Yesterday, I found an enormous spider in my curtains.

FLORINE: The country has to be populated by animals, since people, necessarily, are in the city.

CELINDA: It seems to me that my flesh burns. I'm afraid of being struck by a beam of sunlight if I water the flowers in the garden without a hat.

FLORINE: Madame's skin is always of an admirable whiteness.

CELINDA: You think so?

FLORINE: It's not like that Rosimene's, with her red tint and her yellow neck. I'd like to have the money she spends on makeup and powder.

CELINDA: I hear Suzon's wooden shoes. She's in a hurry. Something extraordinary must have happened.

(Enter Suzon.)

SUZON: Madame, excuse my entrance like this, without a word of warning, into your beautiful room, as if in a pigsty. There's a handsome gentleman who wishes to speak to you.

FLORINE: Show in the handsome gentleman.

CELINDA: No! No!

FLORINE: It will amuse us. I'll be so happy to see a human face.

(Enter the Duke.)

CELINDA: Heavens! The Duke!

FLORINE: Milord! What? Is it you?

DUKE: Myself, charming savage. I've found you again. It's been three weeks that my secret agents have canvassed the country to ferret you out.

FLORINE: The fact is—we are at the end of the world.

DUKE: You must hate me a lot, naughty girl, for you to expatriate yourself so as not to see me. By the way, here's the diamond you sent me back as if I were a tradesman. A person of quality never takes back what's he has given.

CELINDA: Sir!

FLORINE: Only men of birth behave like that!

DUKE: You have a caprice for this little dandy. It's not worth the bother to flee people for that. A man of wit understands everything. I would have arranged things so as not to meet St. Albin, or rather—better to present him to me and I would have sponsored him, if he had some merit. A pretty woman is allowed to have a philosopher as she is allowed to have a poodle. It doesn't make much difference.

CELINDA: St. Albin knew how to inspire me with love of virtue.

DUKE: Him! I shouldn't speak ill of him, for I'd have the air of a dismissed rival, but this dear gentleman is not what he appears to be—or, as they say in the novels, I am much deceived.

FLORINE: I am of the Duke's opinion. Mr. St. Albin has attractions which are not becoming to a patriarchal and rustic man.

CELINDA: Florine—

DUKE: My dear Celinda, I love you more than you could suspect from my light tone and frivolous manners. I've never spoken to you in high flown phrases, yet I've made sacrifices for you which many a romantic and pompous lover would hesitate to perform—not to mention two or three little duels—so you could crush all your rivals. So that your feminine vanity would not suffer, I've mortgaged my ancestral estates, and your divine beauty has expanded splendidly amidst marvels of luxury and art. This sell-off has made you shine double. And while only speaking of dogs and horses, I've rejoiced in having rectified all the injustice of fate that made you only a queen of the Opera—when you should have been born on a throne.

FLORINE: How the Duke expresses himself—with no debt to fashionable books. I don't like lovers who give their lives for their mistress and who refuse her fifty crowns or leave her for some dull wife.

CELINDA: Dear Duke, oh, if I had known. Alas, it is too late. St. Albin adores me. I must end my days in this retreat, far from the noise of the world, far from success.

DUKE: To renounce your art and glory, for a scribbler who deceives you—I'm sure of it. To let that flabby Rosimene make the boards creak where you so lightly danced—it's unpardonable. The public has such bad taste, it is capable of applauding her.

CELINDA: The crowd often takes indecency for sensuality and simpering for grace.

DUKE: You have only to reappear to send her back to the chorus—which she should never have left.

CELINDA: Why speak of that, since my fate is forever fixed?

DUKE: Those are very solemn words.

SUZON: (entering with a letter in her hand) Madame, here's a letter which a boy gave me for you.

CELINDA: It's St. Albin's writing. What can it mean? He just left. What can he have to tell me? I tremble. Break the seal. Duke, you'll excuse me?

DUKE: Why, of course.

CELINDA: (reading) "My dear Celinda, What I have to tell you is so embarrassing that I've taken the means of informing you by letter. You may call me perfidious, but I was only unwise. Destiny does not want me to be happy according to my heart's vows. A man simple and virtuous, I was born to be happy in the country—but an unforeseeable event has recalled me to the city. You know I was a tutor. My pupil had a sister who often heard my lessons. What can I tell you? Julie, for that is her name, scorning vile prejudices, soon gave in to the sweet seductions of nature—and finds herself in the position of giving a new citizen to the fatherland. Her parents, noticing their daughter's condition, summon me to repair the outrage to her honor. I've been forced to agree to marry her—and they insist on bestowing a dowry on her of one hundred thousand crowns. This is very annoying to me, for I've always professed to scorn riches and ask only for pure milk under a thatched roof, right? Don't wish me ill, Celinda. An imperious destiny compels me. Try to forget me—nothing prevents you from remaining where you are amidst simple pleasures and days exempt from troubles. Goodbye forever, The Unfortunate St. Albin."

CELINDA: The rogue! How he deceived me! Oh, I am choking from anger and misery!

DUKE: This doesn't surprise me. Romantic men are always committing follies with rich heiresses.

FLORINE: He's a scoundrel, a libertine, a hypocrite. I've never told madame, but he always hugged me in the dark corridors, and if I'd wanted to— Happily, I have some principles.

CELINDA: And I was capable of preferring him to you.

DUKE: So much the worse for him if he hasn't resembled your dream.

FLORINE: Now we no longer have any reason to stay in the country—if we were to return a little to see what the conditions of the land are in Paris—

CELINDA: Goodbye—daisies, aromas of green hay, smoke from distant burning leaves—my heart has known pleasures too stimulating to be able to endure your sweet, monotonous chorus.

DUKE: Your bucolic interlude is terminated?

CELINDA: Yes. Give my your hand and escort me.

DUKE: My carriage is right at the turn of the road.

FLORINE: Yea! For a working girl, it's better to have love letters than to milk cows.

(They leave.)

BLACKOUT

A FALSE CONVERSATION

SCENE III.

The foyer of the Opera.

ROSIMENE: This imbecile didn't put water in my watering jug. I nearly fell down flopping. My place was clear and shining like a waxed floor.

DE VANDORE: I'll beat the clown when he comes back.

CHEVALIER: Miss Rosimene is taken with exquisite taste.

ROSIMENE: My shirt costs a thousand crowns. Mr. de Vandore has done wonders.

COMMANDER: We are going to dine with you after the ballet. This morning I sent a hamper of game and the recipe for quail.

ROSIMENE: Oh, I adore quail.

CHEVALIER: (aside) She adores everything.

ROSIMENE: I am not a prude like Celinda. I eat and I drink. It's more gay.

COMMANDER: By the way, what's become of Celinda?

DE VANDORE: She's given herself up to the pleasures of the country and foments cream in a Swiss dairy farm.

COMMANDER: Bad nutrition which ruins the stomach. It's bad enough to suck milk when you're a little kid.

ROSIMENE: I prefer tonics and highly seasoned dishes. After all, Celinda has always had romantic ideas. She had the defect of reading. I ask you, what's the good of that?

CHEVALIER: Rosimene, tonight you have such gusto—such pungency, it's incredible how you've improved.

ROSIMENE: I owe it to my big old Croesus. He pays me for masters of all sorts. I don't receive them, but I give them their wages. It's as if I've taken my lesson.

DE VANDORE: She'll become a Ninon, a Marion Delorme, an Aspasia. We'll make the necessary expenses.

CALL BOY: Madame, they're going to start.

ROSIMENE: Good! Good! The public can wait a bit. I have to get ready. I haven't washed today.

(Celinda and the Duke enter.)

CELINDA: My dear little one, don't get so heated up. Your corsage is decidedly soiled with sweat.

ALL: Celinda!

CELINDA: You are not dancing tonight. I'm taking my role back.

ROSIMENE: That's unworthy, that's horrible. I have rights which I will stand on —and my costume which cost me my eyeballs.

CELINDA: That's Mr. de Vandore's concern.

CHEVALIER: (going to Celinda) Is it to your ghost I speak, Celinda? In any case, no one has ever seen a more graceful shade.

CELINDA: It's indeed me, Chevalier. Commander, I invite you for tonight. We will party like crazy until morning. I will try not to put you to sleep.

COMMANDER: (leaving Rosimene) I will be more awake than a bird of dawning.

CELINDA: Marquis, I have to excuse my wrongs. Before, I slandered your wit and your legs. Come, I will be charming.

MARQUIS: (going to Celinda's side) A smile from your mouth makes one forget stinging words.

CELINDA: (aside) Shall I take her de Vandore from her? No, he's too ugly and too stupid. Let's leave him to her. Clemency sits well on grand souls.

CALL BOY: Madame, it's your turn.

CELINDA: Goodbye, gentlemen. Till later. Duke, come get me after my dance. You will escort me home.

CHEVALIER: I told you that this mawkishness wouldn't last. Good blood cannot lie.

CURTAIN

WIDOW!

by Henri Becque

TRANSLATED AND ADAPTED BY
FRANK J. MORLOCK

CAST OF CHARACTERS

CLOTILDE
ADELE, HER MAID
LAFONT

WIDOW!

A small salon where everything is most Parisian. The shutters are three quarters closed allowing only a weak light to penetrate. Clotilde, dressed in black, features drawn, pensive, is reading some letters she's just received.

CLOTILDE: (reading) "My dear cousin— I understood immediately that you had a serious reason for writing me, and that a misfortune had occurred. I wasn't mistaken. My poor Adolphe. So young and taken so quickly. I hadn't seen my cousin for a long while because he had adopted worldly habits for which he was unprepared and which have certainly shortened his life. But I'd retained a memory of our years of childhood and youth that is still present. He had well fulfilled all that he promised. He was good, industrious, confident. He was, at least, an honest man in a period when they are rare. Excuse me, my dear cousin, if I make you wait for my visit. I no longer find the time to leave my home. I don't complain of it. What can a woman do better than consecrate herself to her husband and children.— Your very devoted, Sophie Martineau."

CLOTILDE: What gall! What a pest that Sophie is!

(taking another letter and reading) "Dear Madame— I learned just now from the short note you kindly wrote me of the death of an excellent man so justly appreciated by all those who knew him. This sad news directing my mind to the past troubled me deeply. It's been eight years since my marriage imposed new obligations on me. I've had to separate a bit abruptly from the comfort of friends who occupied a great place in my heart. Since then, I've often evoked their memory and I always remained grateful for the hours of joy and abandon that I owed them. I wish to hope, dear Madame, that your husband left you in a situation worthy of you. I am not asking you a question; I don't allow myself to do that. It's the vow of a businessman who's only lately become one and who knows that money is a great consolation. If I can be of any use to you, dispose of me freely. You will find me at the Credit Lyonnais every day from three to seven. It's there my friends are certain of meeting me and accustomed to address letters to me. Believe, I beg you, dear Madame, in all my regrets for he who is no more. Accept the homage of my devotion and respect.— Albert Crisier, Administrative Assistant."

CLOTILDE: An errand boy! But he remembers—that's something.

ADELE: (entering) Mr. Lafont, Madame.

CLOTILDE: Show him in.

LAFONT: (entering, soberly dressed; going to her tenderly, in a soft voice) How are you?

CLOTILDE: Very tired. And you?

LAFONT: I haven't lived for the last two days. The thought that you were here, alone, without anyone who loves you, while this unfortunate—

CLOTILDE: You are good, I know it.

LAFONT: I sent a wreath. You received it?

CLOTILDE: Yes.

LAFONT: Was it good?

CLOTILDE: Very nice, I thank you.

LAFONT: What time did he die?

CLOTILDE: Around seven o'clock

LAFONT: Did he suffer much?

CLOTILDE: Moderately.

LAFONT: Did he speak of me?

CLOTILDE: Yes.

LAFONT: In good terms.

CLOTILDE: In excellent terms.

LAFONT: Dear Adolphe! He never suspected anything?

CLOTILDE: Did he know!

LAFONT: What did he say to you about me?

CLOTILDE: Much later. I'll tell you all that some other day. I'm going to leave.

(gesture by Lafont) I am going to spend a month with my mother-in-law.

LAFONT: Alone?

CLOTILDE: I won't be alone with my mother-in-law.

LAFONT: And your children?

CLOTILDE: I'd like to take them with me. On the other hand, perhaps it wouldn't be wise to interrupt their studies.

LAFONT: Stay in Paris. Your presence may be necessary.

CLOTILDE: You think so?

LAFONT: Certainly.

CLOTILDE: I will see. My mother-in-law is arriving tonight. We will decide this question together.— Did I ever mention a cousin of my husband, Madame Martineau?

LAFONT: Possibly. I don't recall. Why?

CLOTILDE: I was stupid enough to write her myself announcing Adolphe's death. She just replied to me with a letter, very dry, very perfidious in which she lets me understand that it was I, by leading my husband into the world, who caused his death. What are we coming to, my God! My poor husband, what would he have done with relatives like Mr. and Mrs. Martineau? If I have something to reproach myself with, that's not it.

LAFONT: You have nothing to reproach yourself with.

CLOTILDE: Be quiet.

ADELE: (entering) Here are some letters for Madame.

CLOTILDE: Give them to me.

(after glancing at them) This one is from a person

who is distasteful. I don't know why.

LAFONT: Madame Beaulieu!

CLOTILDE: Exactly.

(after having read the letter with a half smile) What a child that Pauline is. She's always making fun of herself.

LAFONT: Show me her letter, would you?

CLOTILDE: Never.

LAFONT: It's true I don't like her, young Madame Beaulieu. I can't understand this infatuation you have for her. You lost your husband. This one makes you laugh and you approve of her.

CLOTILDE: I don't approve of her.

LAFONT: If I allowed myself the most inoffensive joke you wouldn't find enough reproaches to make me.

CLOTILDE: It's not the same thing. Pauline didn't know how to talk to my husband. They spoke to each other only once a year. Whereas, Adolphe and you, you've been linked since college and you never left each other. Adolphe had a deep affection for you and demonstrated it with his last breath.

LAFONT: What did he say to you about me?

CLOTILDE: You want to know it?

LAFONT: Certainly.

CLOTILDE: So be it. Almost an hour before he died my husband felt much better. He no longer suffered. He took my hands, he spoke to me of his business, of the money he had that I would get when he was no longer. He was very touching at that moment. He had nothing to say. He looked at me and added: "You are going to find yourself in a delicate situation with all your needs and two children to raise. Remarry, that would be the wisest thing. You get on very well with Lafont. He's a man of heart and a smart fellow. If he gets the idea to marry you, you ought to accept him."

LAFONT: He said that?

CLOTILDE: I am repeating his words to you verbatim.

LAFONT: That's funny. I thought that things like that only happened in comedies.

CLOTILDE: Relax, my friend. I won't follow Adolphe's advice. I am not for a moment thinking of remarrying.

(Adele enters)

What's the matter, Adele?

ADELE: They've just brought a wreath on behalf of Mr. Simpson.

(gesture by Lafont)

CLOTILDE: That's nice. Put it with the others.

LAFONT: Are you still seeing that gentleman?

CLOTILDE: I told you a thousand times to the contrary.

LAFONT: Then what's he meddling for?

CLOTILDE: Adele's mistaken. It's Madame Simpson who is sending this wreath. Perhaps she charged her son to do it in her place. No scenes, okay? Think a bit where we are today. You will come to see me tomorrow—after the ceremony.

LAFONT: Certainly.

CLOTILDE: That's fine. You've got to leave me now.

LAFONT: Already?

CLOTILDE: Yes, already. The visitors will arrive any minute; I don't want them to find you installed in my home.

LAFONT: You're right.

(rising and going to her with emotion) Can I see him?

CLOTILDE: If you like. Here. Go this way.

LAFONT: (reaching the door) Till tomorrow!

CLOTILDE: Till tomorrow.

(he goes in to the funeral chamber) To choose between him and my husband, perhaps I'd rather have lost him.

(taking another letter and reading it)

"Madame— Living in the same house as you, I think that my name is not unknown to you. Still, I wouldn't feel myself authorized to write you if we weren't henceforth attached to each other by the identity of our situation and our misfortune. You are a widow, Madame, and I am, too. You adored your husband and mine was everything for me. Baron Formichel had only merits and no faults. With him I knew all the happiness of this world and I've forsaken them after losing him. It will soon be twenty years since my husband died. And I've not ceased for an instant to cherish his memory.—If you'd like to, Madame, one day next week, I will come up to take you and we will go prostrate ourselves before God. The support of religion is very powerful in such cases; it's that which gives me the strength to live and to sacrifice myself. To vanquish my flesh while waiting for the Baron and myself to be reunited for eternity. Allow me, Madame, to call myself your friend.— Rose Christiane Adelaide, Baroness Formichel."

She's mad.

CURTAIN

ABOUT FRANK J. MORLOCK

FRANK J. MORLOCK has written and translated many plays since retiring from the legal profession in 1992. His translations have also appeared on Project Gutenberg, the Alexandre Dumas Père web page, Literature in the Age of Napoléon, Infinite Artistries.com, and Munsey's (formerly Blackmask). In 2006 he received an award from the North American Jules Verne Society for his translations of Verne's plays. He lives and works in México.

www.ingramcontent.com/pod-product-compliance
Lightning Source LLC
LaVergne TN
LVHW011211080426
835508LV00007B/722